ZEN YOGA

Also by Aaron Hoopes

ZEN YOGA: A Path to Enlightenment through Breathing, Movement, and Meditation
(Kodansha International)

***Perfecting Ourselves:
Coordinating Body, Mind and Spirit***
(Turtle Press)

UPDATE: Japan
(Intercultural Press)

The Zen Yoga Daily Warm-Up DVD
(Zen Yoga Press)

Inner Sunrise: A Journey of Deep Relaxation CD
(Zen Yoga Press)

available at: www.artofzenyoga.com

BREATHE SMART
The Secret to Happiness, Health and Long Life

2nd Edition

AARON HOOPES

Zen Yoga Press, Vermont, USA

For more information, to contact the author, or to order additional copies of this book:
> Zen Yoga Press
> 1152 North Rd.
> Vershire, VT, 05079

ISBN   0-9743247-0-1

Library of Congress Control Number: 2003108643
Printed in the United States of America

10 9 8 7 6 5 4 3 2

ACKNOWLEDGMENTS

Thanks to Mom and Dad for all of their support and editing skills.

Thanks to Rita for convincing me that this book needed to be reprinted.

And thanks to Jane for making the original version of this book possible.

If I had to limit my advice on healthier living
to just one tip, it would be simply…
to learn how to breathe correctly.
                    -Andrew Weil, M.D.

--//--

The most effective technique,
To deal with anything, is to use the breath.
If you learn to breathe properly,
All things will fall into place.
                    - Zin the Wandering Sage

--//--

Saying a thing once,
is tantamount to saying it not at all.
There are truths that must be enunciated
Again and again and again
In the same words and in different words
Again and again and again.
                    -Daniel Quinn

Table of Contents

Author's Note

A lot has happened in the five years since this book was first published. I've have been fortunate enough to travel the world teaching and learning and have met so many wonderful people. I have also encountered the countless ways in which modern society challenges us with complex and stressful experiences, It is an honor, therefore to present this material to those who are beginning to seek answers to the deeper questions of life.

The ideas presented here may seem like an oversimplification at times, yet the plain fact is that most of us simply do not breathe effectively. We consign our breathing process a reflexive act at a subsistence level, totally unaware of the potentials that would flow from more breath consciousness.

The intent of this book is to enable anyone to take advantage of the remarkable and surprising benefits conscious breathing brings. We think that there has to be something more complicated, or more expensive that we need to do to feel better. This is just not true. This simple practice can, and will, make a difference in the better health we all seek.

As you read, don't hesitate to begin putting into practice the ideas and exercises you encounter. It will help give them more immediacy and embed them into your mind at a deeper subconscious level. Becoming aware of your breathing as you are reading about breathing allows the mind to connect with the body.

Most importantly, just relax and enjoy exploring and putting into practice some of the thoughts discussed herein. The pursuit of the pleasure and value of breathing, which can enhance your life, should be free of frustration and discomfort.

Breathe to feel good!

In peace.

Aaron Hoopes, 2008

CHAPTER 1

THE

IMPORTANCE

OF

BREATHING

Ancient stories tell of a long-lost fountain hidden away in some remote, forgotten corner of the world. This mythical fountain was reported to flow with magical elixir that cured illness and granted the drinker eternal youth. The driving force behind much of Ponce de Leon's exploration was his obsession with tales of the Fountain of Youth. The idea of living longer has often become a focus for people as they begin to grow older and feel the effects of age and their inevitable mortality. Recently we have been bombarded with remedies both old and new which claim to extend life. From new or improved chemical food supplements to dark chocolate and even laughter, it seems as if everyone has a special method for prolonging life. However, encouraging the body to do what is natural is most often the best one. Ironically, the simple, natural and most beneficial method is often the most neglected as we continue the quest for a healthier more fulfilling life.

In some Eastern philosophies there is a belief that the number of breaths each of us will breathe in our lifetime is already decided and when we reach that number our time is up. It is possible that this could just be some wise sage's unique method for getting his disciples to breathe slower and deeper, but whether it is true or not is irrelevant. The fact remains that we will all reach a point in our lives where we will be unable to draw in another breath. If we take some time to explore and understand a few truths about breathing as a whole, we might just find that the wise old sage is not so far from the mark as we may have thought. We might also find Ponce de Leon's magical elixir is something that has always existed within us, yet we have rarely been able to effectively tap into it.

From a practical angle imagine, for the moment, that the number of breaths you will take in the rest of your life is finite, which, in fact, it is. Does it not make sense to extend those breaths for as long as possible in order to extend life as long as possible? If you can breathe more of them longer, slower and with the utmost quality, you will, in effect, be extending your life. But that is too easy. The ancient sage would probably say something like, "Each breath within each moment contains a lifetime," but cryptic philosophical recursion is of little help to people in the present day who genuinely seek answers to living a longer, healthier and more fulfilling life.

In this book, therefore, I seek to pursue a more pragmatic approach.

Breathing is fundamental to human existence. The human body can survive without food for days or even weeks. It can survive without water for two or three days. However, without oxygen, we die in minutes. The incongruity is that people spend a great part of their lives concerned with eating and drinking, yet for the most part pay very little attention to their breathing.

Breathing is something we do unconsciously. There is no need to pay attention to it since the body takes care of that on its own. But doesn't the body also take care of eating and drinking to some extent? When we are hungry, we eat. When we are thirsty, we drink. Just as when we are out of breath, we breathe.

It's not the same, you may argue. In order to eat you have to physically pick up the food and put it in your mouth. That is a conscious action. Yet I'm sure everyone has experienced the feeling of rampant hunger when we cannot stuff the food in fast enough. The same goes for drinking. Normally we apply conscious effort to bring the liquid to our lips, yet we have all from time to time had that feeling of unquenchable thirst in which we end up guzzling water as if we had never tasted it before. Are these not examples of reflex, if not wholly unconscious, action? We are governed by the body's demands. Of course, when your stomach is sated you regain control, and when your thirst is quenched you can stop drinking, because you know deep within that you have satisfied whatever it was that drove you to that behavior.

But what, in fact, did drive you to that behavior? What caused you to stuff your face until you could hardly put anything else in? What made you gulp down the water as if you were about to die of thirst? At the deepest level the answer is quite simple: the survival instinct, the body's natural drive to preserve and maintain itself.

But you aren't reading this book simply to preserve and maintain yourself, are you?

Health-conscious people today are concerned about their body and general well-being at a much deeper level, seeking secrets to living a healthier and more fulfilling life. If you are reading this book, you are obviously seeking answers as to what you can do to improve the quality of your life. Those of us who are concerned with our health try to eat a healthy diet and avoid junk food. We try to exercise regularly, drink plenty of water and moderate our intake of fats, sugar and alcohol. Why then, should it be any different for our breathing? Just as vegetarians make a conscious effort to adhere to a certain diet and just as some people don't drink alcohol or soft drinks, learning to breathe correctly is a conscious lifestyle choice that is beneficial to the health of the body. *If you are truly concerned with your health and genuinely want to care for your body, you have a tremendous opportunity to satisfy these concerns by learning how to breathe properly and effectively.*

This concept is basic. By learning breathing exercises and practicing them whenever you get an opportunity, your body becomes infused with more life-giving oxygen and vital energy. It begins to feel better. As you feel better you start to breathe easier and fuller, which in turn brings in even more oxygen and energy. It is a positive upwards spiral created simply by breathing consciously. Your body wants to breathe more, all you have to do is let it.

CHAPTER 2

SMART

BREATHING

Subsistence:

> The condition of remaining in existence by maintaining the minimum necessary to support life.

The human body is amazing just because it works. The natural bodily functions go on throughout our lives, and breathing is the most basic of them. We don't have to be conscious of our breathing. The body breathes whether we pay attention to it or not. This normal, everyday unconscious breathing can be defined as subsistence breathing. Subsistence breathing is simply existing by maintaining the minimum breathing necessary to support life.

Subsistence breathing takes place in the upper lungs. It is normally shallow and uses only about one-third of lung capacity. There is nothing wrong with subsistence breathing. It keeps us alive. But is that enough? What happens when we encounter some kind of stress or strain which demands that we have reserves of energy to fall back on? The usual response is heavy, desperate panting until we have "caught" the breath we didn't have. In the face of serious injury, illness, or stress many if not most people restrict their breathing even more than it is restricted during subsistence breathing. The dysfunctional result is to lower their intake of oxygen just when they are most in need of a plentiful supply.

What if we were able to build up a store of energy we could tap into when the need arose, giving us a special source of personal power? Conscious breathing is the key to achieving that power. The first step involves learning about how the body breathes and becoming aware of when its needs are not being met.

Take a "deep" breath and observe what happens. Most likely your upper chest swells out like the Big Bad Wolf about to blow down a house. This may give you a surge of emotional energy or even a feeling of power, but it still meets only your minimum needs for oxygen. The reason for this is because you are only filling the top part of your lungs, the part normally used during subsistence breathing. In contrast, what happens when you exercise vigorously? You start panting and puffing, drawing air as deeply into your lungs as you can while you try to meet the sudden increased need for oxygen caused by the stress of moving the body quickly. This increase in oxygen intake, as it flows through your veins, purifies the system and assists in liberating the energy in the food you eat. It also collects the toxins and poisons generated by your everyday living and expels them as CO_2.

What would happen if you had regular access to this increased amount of oxygen?

Obviously, your body would be supplied with more energy-producing, oxygen-rich blood and its nutrients. In addition, the use of more lung capacity would enable you to expel more toxins and poisons, especially those lurking in the seldom used lower two-thirds of your lungs. This kind of maximization of oxygen intake is what you can achieve through what is called conscious (also abdominal or dynamic) breathing.

I like to call it *smart breathing*.

Don't, by the way, confuse smart breathing with hyperventilation. Hyperventilation is abnormally rapid breathing often associated with anxiety which results in an excessive loss of carbon dioxide from the blood and is definitely not good for you. Conscious breathing is inherently slow, deep and relaxing.

Smart breathing slows down the heartbeat and reduces stress and strain on the muscles of the heart. If you are at all familiar with biorhythms, it should not be a surprise to learn that an electro-encephalogram (EEG) of a person practicing conscious breathing exercises shows a distinct synchronization of alpha waves in different parts of the brain. Alpha rhythm is the prominent EEG wave pattern in an adult who is awake but relaxed with eyes closed. However, the longer conscious breathing is practiced, the smoother and wider the synchronized alpha waves become, even with the eyes open. With smart breathing more oxygen is supplied to the head, enhancing clarity of thought and stimulating brain activity.

There are many other benefits of smart breathing as well. The deep rhythmic expansion and contraction of the muscles around the lungs serves to provide an internal massage to the inner organs of the body. This passive massaging stimulates the liver, kidneys, spleen and other internal organs, bringing vital energy to keep them healthy and functioning properly.

But let's get to the really good news: reaping the benefits of conscious breathing is ridiculously simple.

PAYING ATTENTION

Attention Breathing is a preparatory exercise which focuses your awareness on the natural rhythm of your breath, not to control it but simply to observe it as a bodily function. Most people rarely notice their own breathing habits. It is not something that we consider important. The incongruity is that breathing is what keeps us alive.

Begin by concentrating on the feeling of the body as it breathes. Feel the air as it enters your nostrils. Follow it as it flows down into the lungs and notice how deeply it reaches. Become aware of the rest of your body. Does it take any part in your breathing? Follow your exhalation. Is all the breath in the lungs expelled? Try to feel the used air leaving your body. Notice if there is any tension or stress anywhere.

Don't try to change your breathing during Attention Breathing. Your aim is simply to observe your unconscious breathing habits so you will be able to feel the difference when you actually begin conscious breathing. The awareness of your breathing should eventually become an integral part of your life.

NASAL BREATHING

While there are a number of different ways to breathe, one of the most beneficial for overall health is breathing through the nose. The human body was designed for us to breathe through the nose and take in food and water through the mouth. Of course they are all connected and, in fact, there are times when we must breathe through the mouth, such as when we are out of breath. However, breathing through the nose is of the utmost importance when practicing smart breathing, simply because it facilitates the best possible energy circulation.

Nasal Inhalation

When we breathe in through the nose, there are a series of defense mechanisms that prevent impurities and extremely cold air from entering the body. First, a screen of nose hairs traps dust and other particles that could be harmful to the lungs if we breathe through the mouth. Next, there is a long passage lined with mucus membranes, where excessively cool air is warmed and very fine dust particles that escaped the hair screen are caught. Finally, in the inner nose are glands which fight off bacteria that may have slipped through the other defenses. The inner nose also contains the olfactory organ that gives us our sense of smell, which can detect poisonous fumes that could damage our health if we were to breathe them.

Nasal Exhalation

Breathing out through the nose is seldom regarded with the same significance as breathing in; however, when doing these specific exercises it is important. Think of breathing in and out through the nose as a closed circuit within the body. If you open your mouth, you break the circuit and the energy dissipates.

Indian yogis and Tai Chi masters of China have learned that breathing through the nose allows them to circulate the energy through the body and use it to keep the body warm and vibrant. By breathing through the nose we can generate and concentrate this energy for maximum benefit. In addition breathing out through the nose regulates the levels of oxygen and carbon dioxide in the body. This allows you to practice dynamic breathing without getting light-headed or dizzy.

When breathing through the nose, your tongue should lightly touch the top palate of your mouth. This connection allows the energy to circulate effectively. There is often a light whooshing sound as the air enters and leaves the nose. Cultivate this sound. It aids in concentration during breathing.

Regular practice of Smart Breathing can bring dramatic results in a short period of time. By paying attention to your breathing you can heighten your general self-awareness. You will begin to notice the way you are living and how your body is reacting to the lifestyle choices you make. From there you can move on to learning how to maximize the quality of your breathing. First let's make sure we have the correct posture.

CHAPTER 3

BREATHING

POSTURES

Correct posture is the first prerequisite for performing breathing exercises. Proper alignment facilitates energy flow through the body. If the posture is incorrect, the energy may not flow smoothly and can even become blocked. By maintaining good posture we encourage a healthy flow.

While you can practice breathing exercises anywhere at any time, there are three postures used for basic breathing exercises: standing, sitting and lying down.

STANDING

When standing and breathing, your feet should be separated to the same width as your hips and shoulders. Feet, knees, hips and shoulders all line up. The buttocks should not stick out. Instead, the hips should be slightly tucked under to straighten the lower spine. Feel a lengthening in the back as if a string is drawing your spine upwards from the crown of your head. Keep the knees unlocked so that they remain relaxed. Your shoulders should be loose and let the arms hang down naturally. Tuck your chin in slightly so that it aligns with the navel.

SITTING

When sitting and breathing, alignment of the spine is important. The muscles of the back can quickly become fatigued and make maintaining the posture difficult. It can be very helpful to position your knees below your pelvis. When sitting with the knees higher than the pelvis the lumbar region of the spine moves backward and the upper torso becomes compressed and curved, making effective breathing rather difficult. Placing the knees below the pelvis allows the hips to rotate forward and positions the upper torso straight and tall. This gives the lungs maximum space for expansion and there is a clear and unobstructed pathway for the breath to move through the body. It can be useful to place a cushion under your buttocks while letting your knees fall to the floor. This will raise your hips higher than your knees while providing some comfort.

LYING DOWN

When lying down and breathing it is best to be on your back, face up. In this position, however, it is easy to fall asleep since the body becomes very relaxed. The feet should be shoulder-width apart and gently flop to the outside. Place a pillow under your knees if you feel pressure on your lower spine.

During all breathing exercises, keep your mouth closed with the tip of your tongue connected to the roof of your mouth. Your eyes may be open, closed, or half-closed. If open, they should be relaxed and unfocused. It is mostly a matter of individual comfort. Start with your eyes closed and adjust as needed.

CHAPTER 4

ABDOMINAL

BREATHING

Abdominal Breathing – also called deep dynamic breathing or belly breathing – is the basic method for learning and practicing smart breathing habits. Regular practice brings quick, tangible results. It is simple to learn and difficult to do incorrectly. However, it may seem a little confusing at the beginning if you are not used to focusing your attention on your breath. The truth is that it is the way babies naturally breathe. Unfortunately, like so many of the virtues we exhibit as children, we lose the skill as we grow up. Next time you have a chance to observe a sleeping baby, notice the rhythmic rise and fall of its abdomen. Babies practice belly breathing unconsciously!

Abdominal Breathing is about filling the lungs completely, instead of using only the upper chest or the top third of the lungs. Abdominal Breathing seeks to expand lung capacity by starting from the lowest part of the lungs and gradually expanding and contracting from the bottom. The focus, therefore, is directed to the body's center of gravity located at the abdomen, an area roughly three-finger widths below the navel. This type of breathing may seem backwards at first, but you will soon become comfortable with it and realize it is quite natural.

There are actually two different methods of Abdominal Breathing: Normal Abdominal Breathing (NAB) and Reverse Abdominal Breathing (RAB).

NORMAL ABDOMINAL BREATHING

NAB is an energy-generating breathing practice. It is the method of breathing that you should be practicing most often. Start in whichever posture (standing, sitting or lying down) you feel most comfortable. Inhale through your nose. Expand your abdomen gradually by lightly pushing out and down as the oxygen fills the lower lung cavity. Try to achieve a gentle and smooth expansion in time with the inhalation. When your abdomen is full, exhale through your nose and pull your belly gently back into your body, compressing the lungs from the bottom. With each inhalation your stomach expands, with each exhalation it contracts. Don't expand or contract your upper chest; instead, feel as if you are drawing the air deep into the lower part of your body. Repeat ten times, filling yourself to maximum capacity and emptying completely with each breath.

This process is one of visualization. You are not actually breathing into your abdomen. You are visualizing what it feels like. What is actually happening is that the extension of the stomach muscles creates a vacuum which draws the lungs deeper down into the chest cavity allowing the lungs to fill to their maximum expansion. Regular practice of NAB strengthens these muscles and gives the lungs a measure of elasticity which can increase their overall capacity.

Sometimes it is helpful to place your hands on your belly, just below your navel during NAB. This has the immediate benefit of giving you a focal point to concentrate on. It also grounds you and centers your attention on the breath. It is very easy for the mind to wander when doing deep breathing and the benefit is lost. Concentrate on the spot of your body where your hands are. As you continue your breathing, you should begin to feel warmth beneath your hands. This is the intrinsic energy that you generate as you breathe.

Placing the hands on the stomach can also help you to get into the rhythm of breathing by exaggerating the rise and fall of the abdominal cavity. During exhalation the added weight of the hands can serve to press the stomach lightly and help you to exhale more completely.

REVERSE ABDOMINAL BREATHING

RAB is a deep breathing practice that is the complete opposite of NAB, reversing the natural flow of the breath and increasing its natural vitality. RAB is often practiced by martial arts students since it strengthens the stomach muscles and calls for focused concentration on the abdomen. It is a breathing method that is especially valuable when we need an immediate and/or new source of strength or energy. Martial artists, when fighting, frequently yell as they complete a strike. This is an example of power generation during RAB. If you have ever watched professional tennis you probably have noticed how many players grunt or yell as they strike the ball. They too are deriving their power from RAB.

Try this: blow up a balloon while keeping one hand on your stomach. You will notice that your abdomen naturally expands instead of contracting during exhalation. This is also true if you try to push a heavy object, such as a car that has run out of gas. In order to effectively use the power of your breath, your stomach should naturally expand as you push out.

Again, start in whatever posture you feel most comfortable. Inhale through the nose and slowly draw the abdomen in and up. Your upper chest will naturally expand as oxygen fills your lungs. As you inhale, feel as if you are contracting the whole abdominal area. Don't be overanxious and squeeze too forcefully. Instead, focus on maintaining a smooth and relaxed feeling within the body. When the lungs are at their maximum capacity, slowly and smoothly exhale through the nose. As you exhale, release the abdomen and push it out and down. Imagine that while the air is leaving through the nose the vital energy is filling up the abdominal cavity. Repeat ten times, filling the upper chest and lungs to maximum capacity and then pushing out the stomach as far as possible during exhalation.

Like normal deep breathing, RAB is also a method of visualization. Try to feel the vital energy entering the abdomen with each exhalation. Use the lungs to their maximum capacity. Consistent practice of RAB helps with balance and centering of the body as well as generating power in the lower body.

A regular schedule of NAB and RAB can quickly get you on the way to feeling healthy and energized. Practice NAB in the morning for a few minutes before you get up to face the day. It is an ideal time to energize the body. Practice RAB during the day to keep you going. At night, after a long day, a few minutes of NAB breathing can quickly calm you down and facilitate a peaceful sleep. When you are comfortable with the two phases of abdominal breathing, proceed to the breathing exercises.

CHAPTER 5

BREATHING

EXERCISES

We breathe in a continuous cycle. The air comes in, circles through the body and flows out. It is important to become fully aware of this natural cycle. By following it consciously, breathing becomes calmer, deeper and more rhythmic.

The following exercises will enable you to fully understand the breathing cycle. While they may seem very simple, effective breathing is about putting these basic ideas into actual practice. Knowing how to do it is not enough. You must actually practice. There are four parts to each breathing cycle. The two main ones are inhalation and exhalation which have been our focus so far. The first part of this exercise section is going to concentrate on the other two aspects of the breathing process, retention and suspension, which are often overlooked. Next we will put it all together for the complete cycle of breathing. Finally we will look at ways of teaching ourselves to remember to breathe.

RETENTION

Retention is basically holding your breath. We have all done this at times in our lives without realizing the hidden benefit it brings. It is not meant to put a strain on the body and should only be practiced for short periods of time. The purpose is to give the lungs a chance to fully process the oxygen that we breathe in before exhaling. By holding the breath, every corner of the body is able to receive vital energy. Retaining the breath inside the body for a moment before exhaling also gives the body a chance to pause and prepare itself for breathing out. It slows down the breathing cycle, making each breath important and meaningful.

Begin practicing retention after having engaged in NAB for a few minutes. Start by taking in a deep breath through the nose. When the lungs are completely full, stop and hold. Hold the breath for a count of five - modify the count to the way your body feels. When you reach five, slowly release the breath through the nose as you exhale. The exhalation should be smooth and natural. Do not empty the lungs quickly. That defeats the whole point of the exercise. You are trying to build up strength in the muscles surrounding the lungs. Gradual release of the air forces the muscles to control their contraction. A slow, smooth exhalation also relaxes the rest of the body as tension is allowed to dissipate gently.

SUSPENSION

Suspension is similar to retention except it is pausing the breathing cycle when all the breath is out of the body. Suspension is a little more difficult than retention. At some point or other in our lives we have all had a chance to practice retention. Whether it was trying to hold our breath underwater or simply avoiding an unpleasant smell, retention is something we are familiar with. Suspension is different. It can, in fact, feel completely alien. The natural reaction to breathing out is to immediately breathe in. In this exercise we seek to stay void for a moment before allowing the body to inhale.

When practicing suspension it is important to stay void for only a few moments. By suspending the breath we are letting the body use up all the remaining oxygen left over from the last inhalation. Once this is accomplished and we next inhale, the new oxygen enters the body and travels to all parts of the body filling it with tremendous energy. By suspending the breath we force the body to crave new oxygen, thereby assuring the fresh air is used to its maximum potential when we finally do breathe in.

To begin, after having done some relaxing NAB, exhale completely through the nose. Continue to blow out all the air in the lungs until they feel totally empty. Stop and hold the breath out for a mental count of five (modify the count to suit your body). At first this may seem impossible as the body's desire to inhale is overpowering, but stay calm. When the five-count is finished, slowly begin to breathe in through the nose, filling the lungs up from the bottom in a slow and smooth inhalation. Don't panic and suck the air in too fast. By breathing in slowly and smoothly, the fresh oxygen fills the body to maximum capacity for maximum benefit.

COMPLETE CYCLE BREATHING

Complete Cycle Breathing (CCB) is a dynamic breathing exercise that integrates Abdominal Breathing with retention and suspension. It is most beneficial to practice CCB with NAB though you can experiment with RAB once you are comfortable with it. Regular practice of CCB cleans and invigorates the lungs while expanding lung capacity. It also naturally slows down your unconscious breathing pattern and makes it smoother and more regular. In addition, complete-cycle breathing maximizes oxygen intake, reduces stress, and causes oxygen-rich blood to flow more readily to the extremities.

At the start, it is best if CCB is practiced from a lying-down position so concentration can be placed on the exercise without concern for posture.

The exercise itself consists of four separate steps: inhalation, retention, exhalation, suspension, repeated in a long, smooth cycle.

Complete Inhalation

Inhale through the nose slowly in long, smooth and continuous breaths. Expand the lower abdomen, pushing out and down as if you were starting abdominal breathing. But now, once your abdomen is full, continue inhaling and expand the chest, filling the upper lungs. Raise the collarbone and shoulders as you continue inhaling. Expand it into the throat and the nose. Fill up the body completely. Stop.

Complete Retention

Hold the breath in. Relax and try to bring your attention to the fullness of your body. Feel the circulation of the oxygen-rich blood throughout your body. Continue to hold the breath in for a count of five. There should be no stress or strain while retaining your breath.

Complete Exhalation

Exhale through the nose slowly in long, smooth and continuous breaths. Begin by contracting your lower abdomen. Feel as if you are drawing it in and up. Continue to exhale by squeezing the air from your lungs and chest. Lower the collarbone and shoulders. Empty the air from your throat and nose. Empty it all out completely. Stop.

Complete Suspension

Hold the breath out. Relax and try to bring your attention to the emptiness of your body. Feel the void within, like an empty balloon waiting to be filled. Continue to suspend breathing for a count of five. There should be no stress or strain within the body.

Repeat

Cn the next inhalation don't gasp for air. The natural reaction to suspension is a rapid intake of breath. However, try to breathe in calmly and smoothly just as before. This allows fresh oxygen to reach the remote corners of the body. Feel the air reaching far beyond your abdomen, filling every part of your body like an expanding balloon. Notice the sensations throughout your body as the new oxygen is brought in.

Practicing CCB takes very little time, about two minutes if done properly. See if you can build it into your daily routine. Try to do the complete cycle three times per day. Once you are comfortable, gradually work up to more. Set yourself the goal of eventually doing the complete set of five or ten.

As with all breathing exercises, if it is difficult for you to retain or suspend breathing for a count of five, begin with a count of two or three and build up. Never hold the breath in or out for longer than feels comfortable. We are trying to make the body feel better, not worse. As with all exercises, get to know what works for your own body.

Recap: CCB Exercise

1 - Inhalation

2 - Retention

3 - Exhalation

4 - Suspension

5 - Repeat

CHAPTER 6

REMEMBER

TO

BREATHE

The biggest problem we face when beginning breathing training is that the body doesn't need us to be aware of the breathing we do just to stay alive. This is fine, but it does make it easy to rely on subsistence breathing patterns. So the challenge becomes remembering to spend some time every day breathing slowly and deeply. During the typical day there are numerous opportunities to practice smart breathing. We have all spent time standing in lines at the store, sitting in the doctor's waiting room or stuck in traffic at rush hour. These are ideal times to devote a few moments to deep breathing. Situations such as this are usually annoying and promote stress. Why not use them to cultivate the habit of deep breathing which is calming and can take you down the road to happier, healthier living?

THE CONNECTED BREATH

There are many ways people remind themselves of things they need to do. One of the best is what I call "The Connected Breath." In this technique you connect your breathing to an action or event that occurs frequently during the day. Get in the habit of associating deep breathing with these events and actually taking one or more breaths when you engage in them. For instance:

- Every time you look at your watch
- Whenever you get into your car

- Before brushing your teeth
- Just before you answer the phone
- Just as you get in or out of bed
- Between clicks of the remote
- Each time you pull open a door
- While you wait for a webpage to load

This list could go on forever. There are hundreds of things you do in daily life that are perfect moments to become aware of your breathing. Choose one or two or make up some others and see if you can get into the habit of remembering to breathe.

Try to compile reminders as you go. Eventually you will begin remembering to breathe at other times of the day and be literally able to fill your life with the new energy and the happy, healthy feelings generated by it.

CHAPTER 7

STRESS,

WEIGHT LOSS

AND BREATHING

Most of us understand that a healthy diet and exercise are vitally important to effective weight loss. However, it may come as a surprise to find out that despite your best efforts, in addition to all the other problems stress brings, it may also be working against you to prevent weight loss. Fortunately, once you understand how it works, there are a couple of simple things you can do to reverse the problem.

There are two systems that control the internal functioning of the body: the parasympathetic nervous system (PNS) and the sympathetic nervous system (SNS). The PNS is concerned with resting and digestion. When you are relaxed, the PNS allows blood pressure to decrease, slows the heartbeat and facilitates your digestive process.

The SNS, on the other hand, is primarily concerned with the "fight or flight" response within your body. The "fight or flight" response is an important stimulus that is triggered when you are startled or surprised. At these times blood pressure increases, your heart beats faster, and your digestive process slows down. When this happens the adrenal glands enlarge and begin to secrete large quantities of adrenal cortical hormones which suppress inflammatory responses and mobilize the body's energy reserves. It is like putting the body on red alert. As the body diverts all of its resources toward survival, your body's natural healing mechanisms are scaled back.

Cortisol is a hormone that is produced in the adrenal cortex. It plays an important role in regulating blood sugar, managing energy production, dealing with inflammation, and maintaining the immune system. Too little cortisol can cause chronic fatigue and exhaustion. Too much cortisol may cause weight gain. Since its role is to provide energy to the body, cortisol can cause an increase in appetite which may lead to overeating. In addition, elevated cortisol levels have been found to cause fat to be deposited in the abdominal region.

During the "fight or flight" response of the sympathetic nervous system, cortisol levels are elevated as a reaction to the stress of the situation. The origin of the stress is irrelevant. The adrenal glands are not concerned with the type of stress that triggers the release of cortisol. It can be physical, environmental, chemical, or imaginary.

In the distant past, the "fight or flight" response worked very well when humans were dealing with creatures that wanted to eat us for dinner. But as the human race has ascended to the top of the food chain, those dangers have eased. Unfortunately, the fast pace of life and the frenetic energy modern society calls forth keeps all of us in a state of constant stimulation. The stress that this creates as we battle traffic jams, stand in line at the post office, and watch rapidly flickering images on the television, resembles the same physiological responses as having to run for your life. Since these stimuli don't stop or go away, the body is left with chronically high levels of cortisol. If you are dealing with stress on a daily basis, it is quite probable that your sympathetic nervous system is in a constant state of stimulation.

Most of us today realize that stress is a principal cause of many of our health problems. The best way to deal with stress is by changing our behavior and being more selective about the situations we put ourselves in. The interesting thing about stress is that it feeds on itself, and a little bit of stress can easily magnify into a serious dysfunction.

Deep breathing creates a harmonious rhythm within the body, reducing stress and strain on the muscles of the heart and slowing down the heartbeat. The rhythmic expansion and contraction of the muscles used in breathing improves muscle elasticity while increasing circulation of blood through the body. In addition, the deep rhythmic expansion and contraction of the diaphragm and muscles around the lungs not only enhances their strength, but massages the body's internal organs. Creating a regular conscious breathing practice can help you manage your stress levels and ease the sympathetic nervous system's hold on you.

As your system relaxes, your adrenal glands regulate the amount of cortisol that is being secreted. In this manner, by simply learning to breathe and relax, you can release tension and get your body working at its best. Allow the breath to guide you towards your ideal weight.

Of course, breathing is just one part of an overall healthy lifestyle. Negative lifestyle choices such as smoking or poor diet need to be addressed in order to fully experience the benefits of the practice.

CHAPTER 8

CONCLUSION

Breathing is something that we often take for granted. Yet it can become something much more profound if we give it the attention it deserves. Continue practicing the exercises presented here and begin connecting to what you are feeling within your body. You now have a tool that is available to you any time stress begins to build up. Realize that the magical elixir so many have searched for has been with us the whole time. Allow your body to enjoy the benefits of the extra oxygen and energy you are giving it. The expanded oxygen content of your lungs simply makes you feel good. Give your body a chance to recognize this and soon it will crave more. You will often find your body wanting to breathe deeper and, by fulfilling that desire, you will be on the upward spiral to feeling great!

When you are ready to move forward, I invite you to explore Zen Yoga. Zen Yoga is the combination of different practices from various Eastern health and fitness traditions. The philosophy of Zen Yoga is embodied in the graceful movements of Chinese Tai Chi, the energized breathing of Qigong, the calm serenity of Japanese Zen and the peaceful stretching and breathing exercises of Shanti Yoga. It is this system of gentle movement which will facilitate an even deeper experience of the breath as the body opens to the flow of this life-giving force.

By putting Zen and Yoga together we create a holistic system that unites all aspects of the human self by meeting the fundamental needs of physical health, mental clarity and spiritual peace. This integration fosters flexibility, health, vitality, creativity, and peace of mind. Zen Yoga is not about what you **can't** do. It has been designed to be accessible to anyone regardless of their age, level of fitness, state of health or spiritual development.

Most of us are seeking more from life. Unfortunately, the distractions of the world often get in the way of our search. Practicing Zen Yoga brings us back into balance and provides an opportunity to feel happy, healthy and alive.

May your journey be peaceful and profound.

ABOUT THE AUTHOR

Aaron Hoopes is the founder of Zen Yoga. He has studied the martial arts, Eastern philosophy, and alternative medicine in the United States, Australia, and Japan for over twenty-five years. He spent a number of years in Japan studying under the chief instructor of the Japan Karate Association. Aaron also studied Shanti (peace) Yoga, Tai Chi, Qigong and Meditation in Australia. He has taught hundreds of classes and workshops around the world.

Aaron's Zen Yoga teachings are available to anyone regardless of age, fitness level, or state of health. Everyone has a body that can breathe and move. Zen Yoga provides simple methods for circulating the life force energy through the body.

Zen Yoga online training is open to anyone who seeks a deeper understanding of this work for their own knowledge. It also provides the basis of certification for those wishing to become Zen Yoga instructors.

Please visit www.artofzenyoga.com for more information.

We want your feedback!
For more information or to order extra copies of

BREATHE SMART

contact us at:

1152 North Rd.
Vershire, VT 05079

Phone: 860-805-6551

Email: breathe@artofzenyoga.com

Website: www.artofzenyoga.com